FOLLOW US ON
INSTAGRAM
@KindergartenEducation

THIS NOTEBOOK BELONGS TO:

# MORE BOOKS BY SMART KIDS NOTEBOOKS

(SCAN THE QR CODE OR VISIT: bit.ly/smartkidsnotebooks)

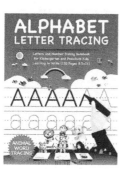

# I SEE 0 EGGS IN THE NEST

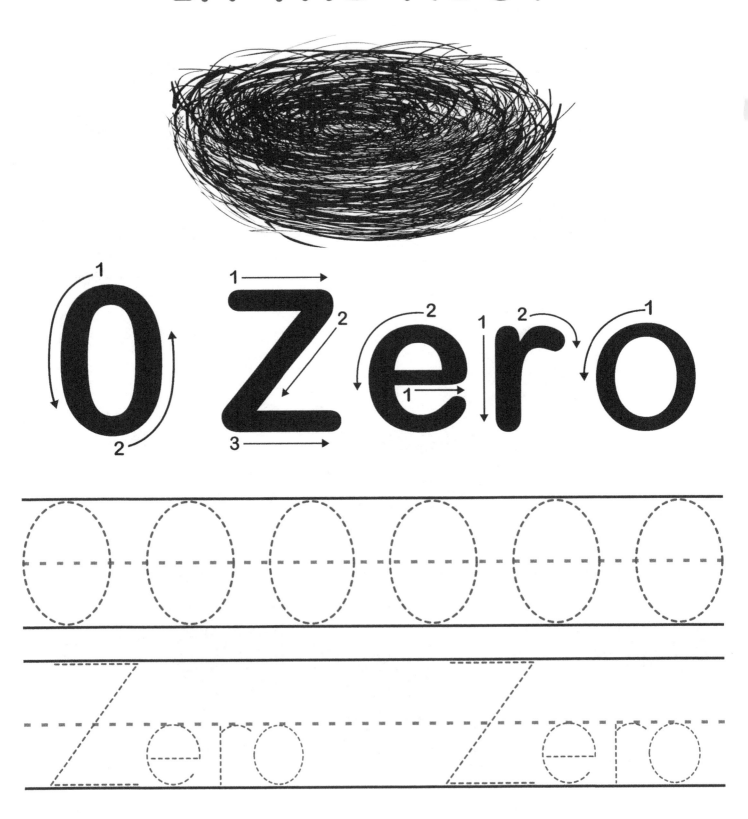

# I SEE 1 BEAR

# I SEE 2 FOXES

# I SEE 3 COWS

# I SEE 4 STORKS

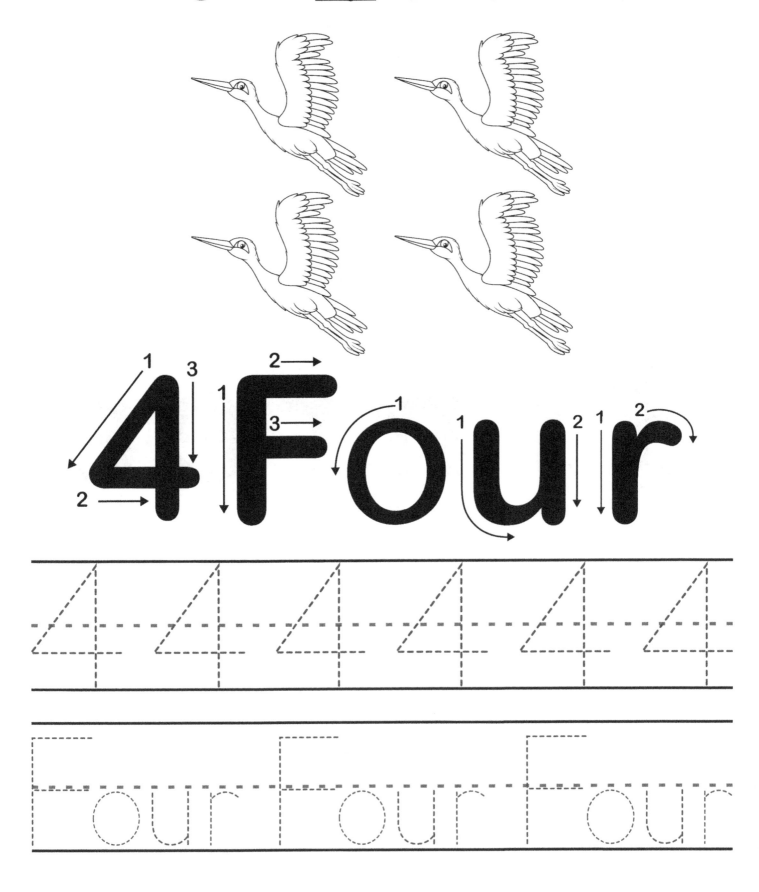

# I SEE 5 PIGS

# I SEE 6 CAMELS

# I SEE 7 SHEEP

# I SEE 8 MICE

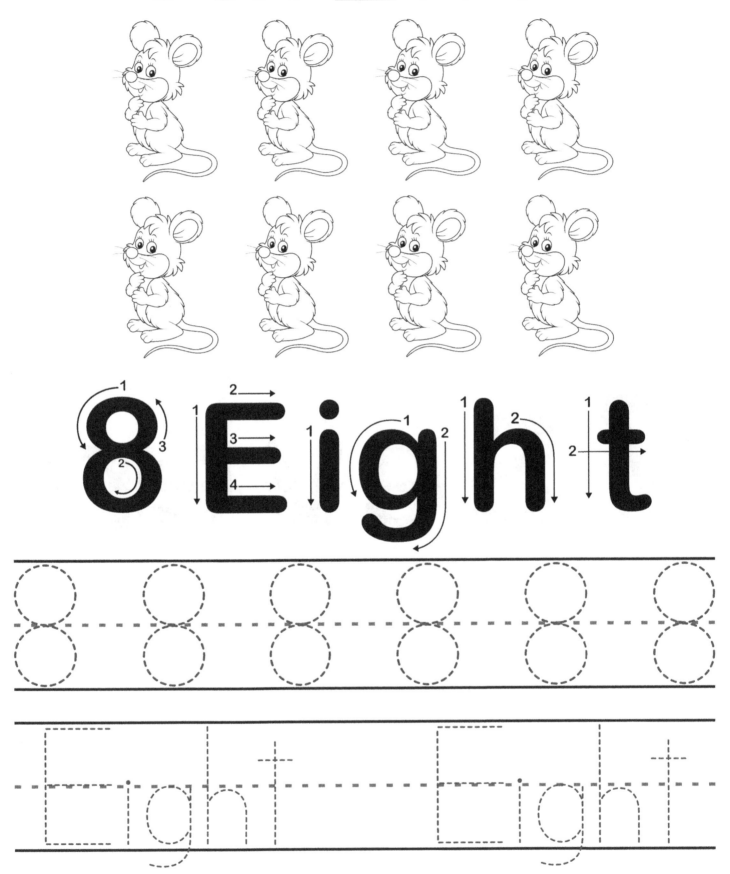

# I SEE 9 BEAVERS

# I SEE 10 GEESE

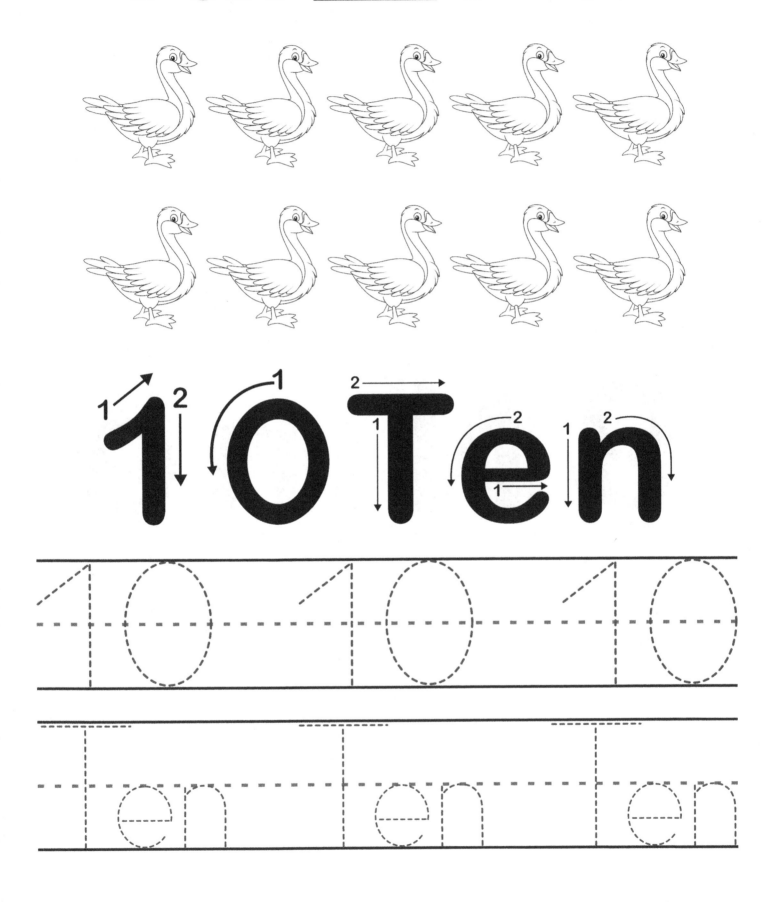

# I SEE 11 FROGS

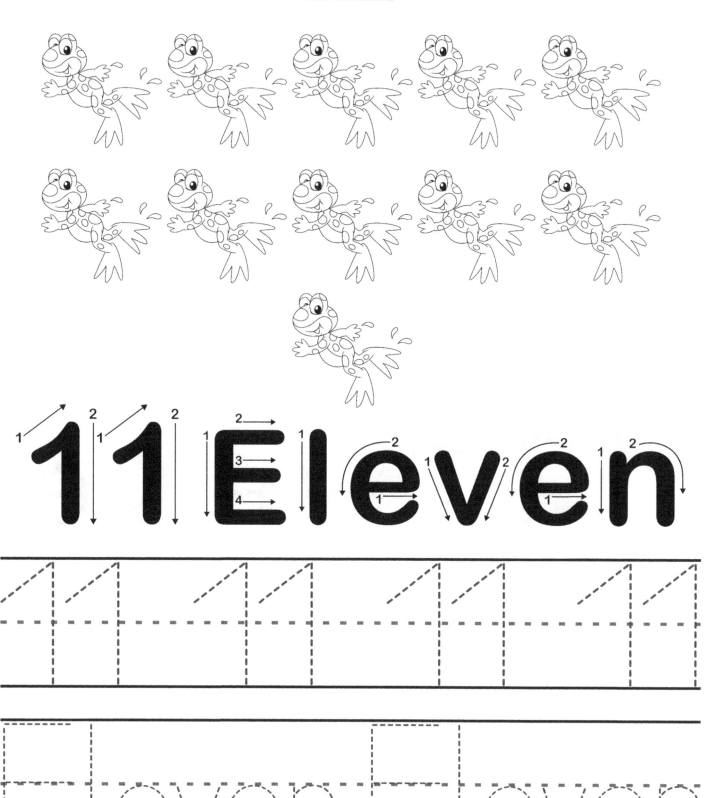

# I SEE 12 SEALS

# I SEE 13 SPARROWS

# I SEE 14 TURKEYS

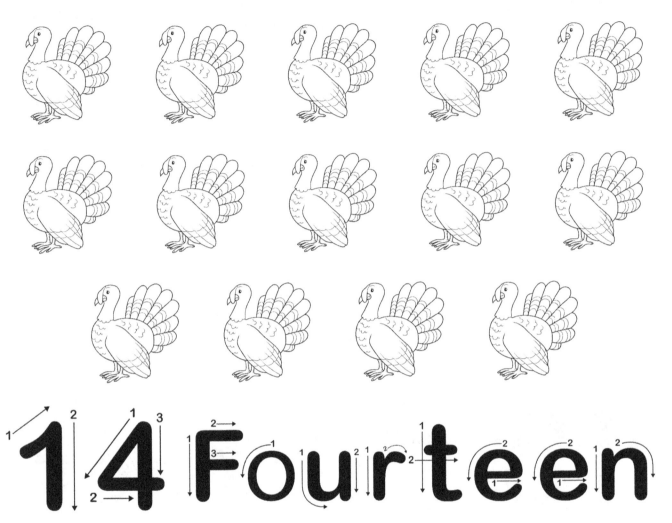

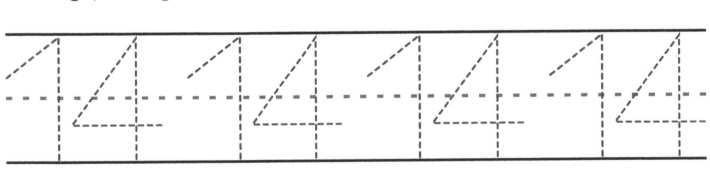

# I SEE 15 DEER

15 Fifteen

15 15 15 15 15

Fifteen Fifteen

# I SEE 16 IGUANAS

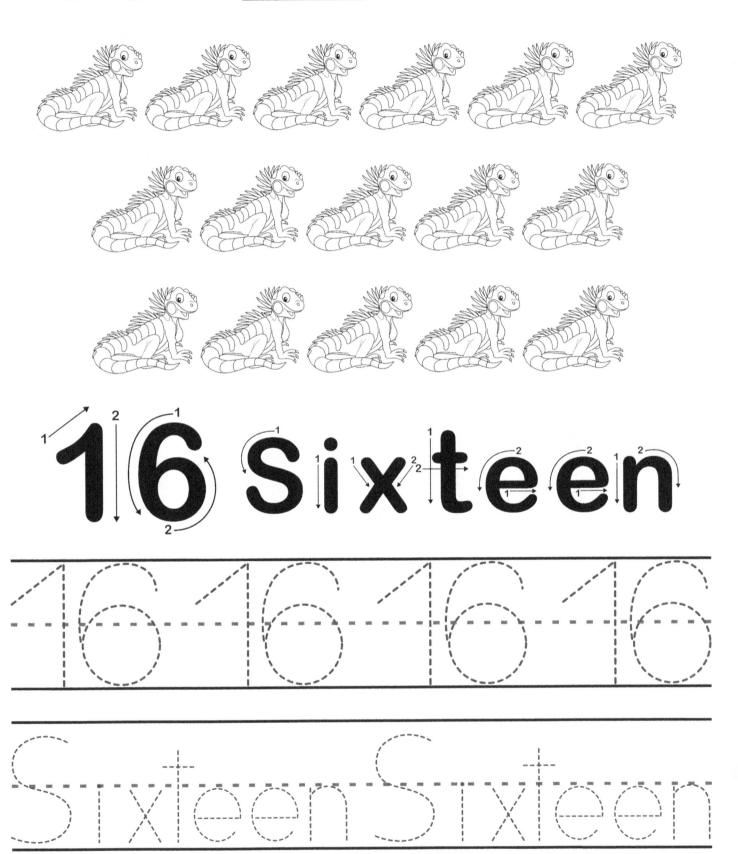

16 Sixteen

# I SEE 17 EMUS

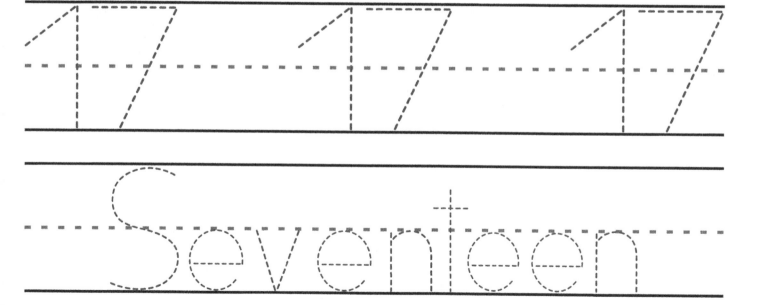

# I SEE 18 RHINOS

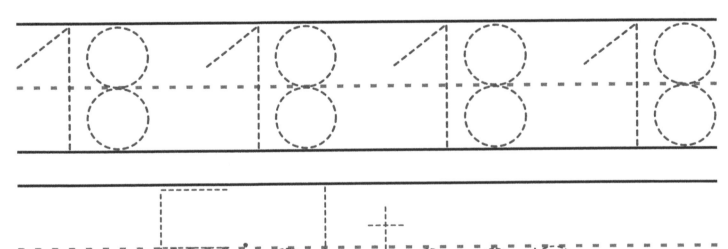

# I SEE 19 HORSES

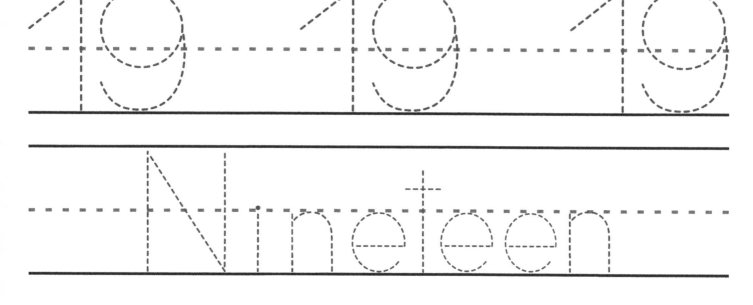

# I SEE 20 DOGS

# LET'S RECAP THE NUMBERS

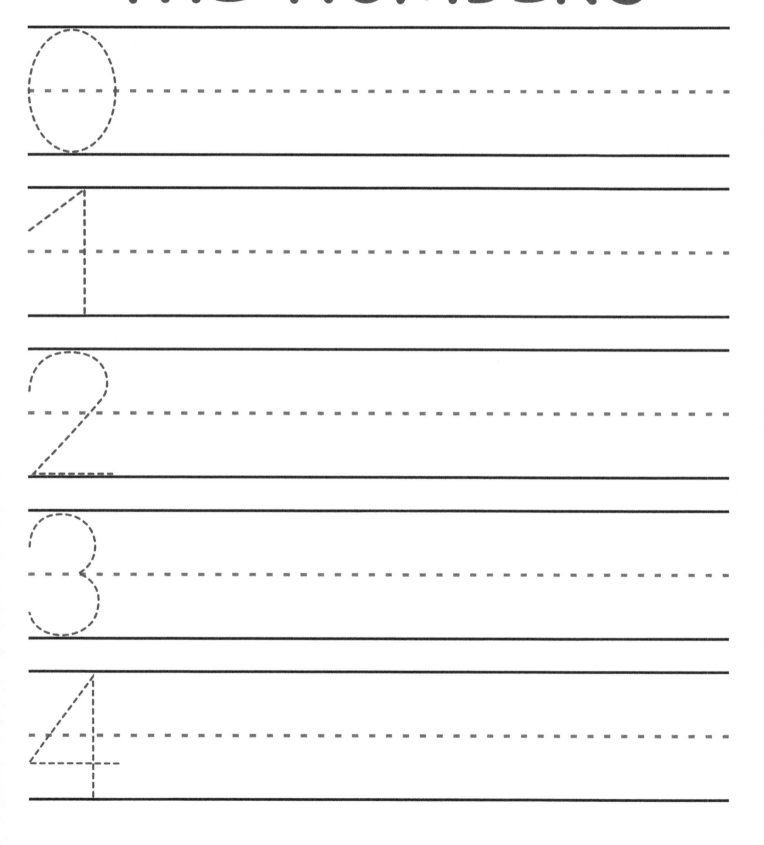

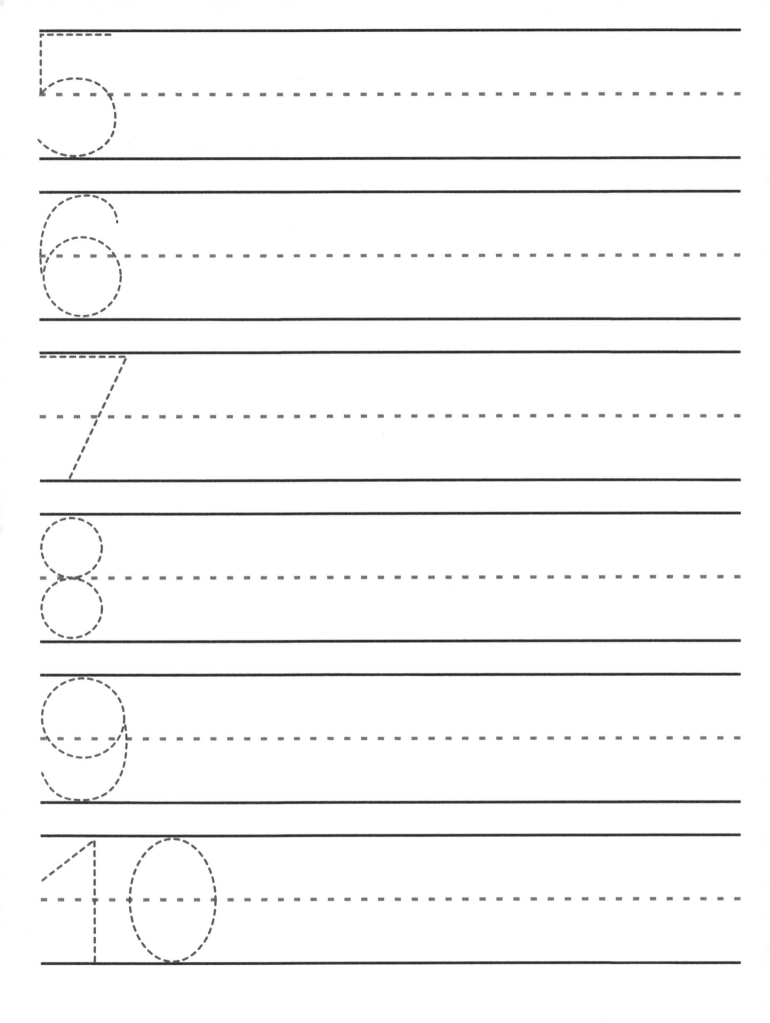

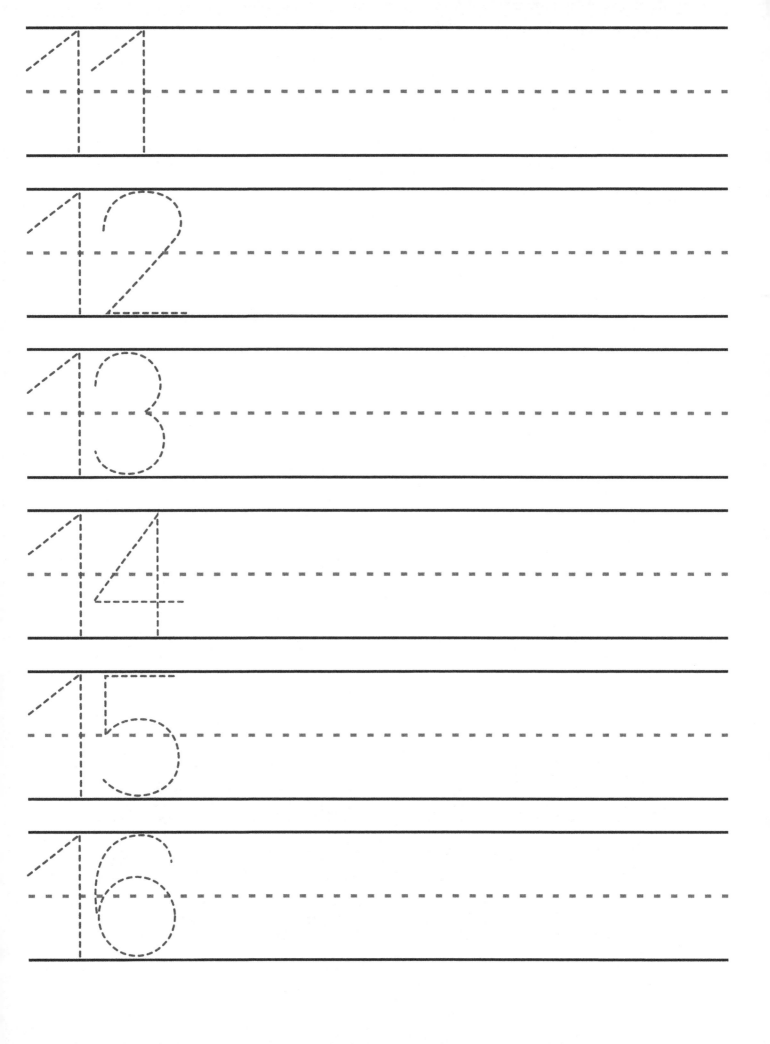

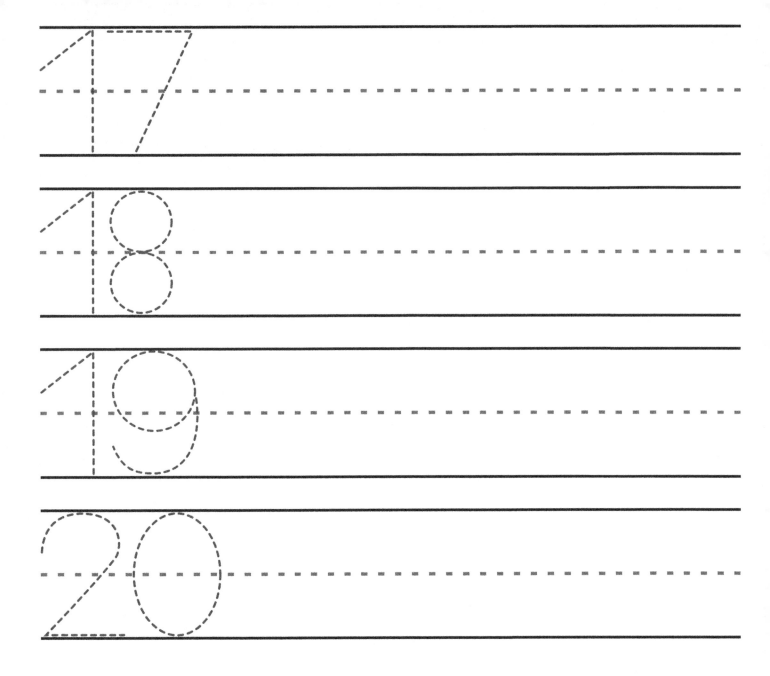

# WELL DONE!
## ARE YOU READY FOR
## THE NEXT CHALLENGE?

# CONNECT THE DOTS TO DRAW THE IMAGE

ANSWER

# CONNECT THE DOTS TO DRAW THE IMAGE

ANSWER

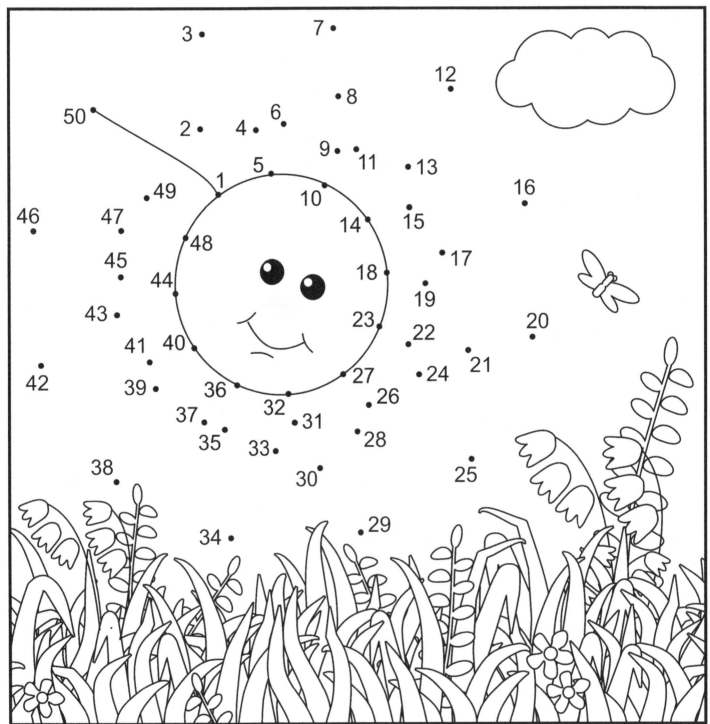

# CONNECT THE DOTS TO DRAW THE IMAGE

ANSWER

# COUNT AND CIRCLE THE CORRECT ANSWER

# COUNT AND CIRCLE THE CORRECT ANSWER

| 9 | 4 | 7 |
|---|---|---|

| 6 | 1 | 5 |
|---|---|---|

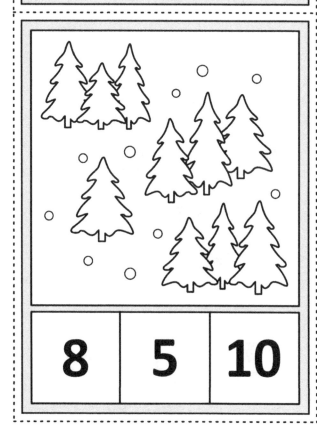

| 8 | 5 | 10 |
|---|---|---|

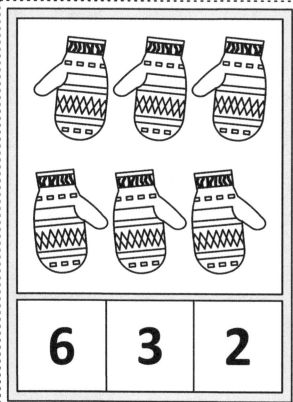

| 6 | 3 | 2 |
|---|---|---|

# COUNT AND CIRCLE THE CORRECT ANSWER

| 4 | 5 | 3 |
|---|---|---|

| 7 | 8 | 6 |
|---|---|---|

| 3 | 7 | 1 |
|---|---|---|

| 2 | 3 | 9 |
|---|---|---|

# COUNT AND CIRCLE THE CORRECT ANSWER

| 2 | 1 | 3 |
|---|---|---|

| 6 | 5 | 7 |
|---|---|---|

| 4 | 5 | 2 |
|---|---|---|

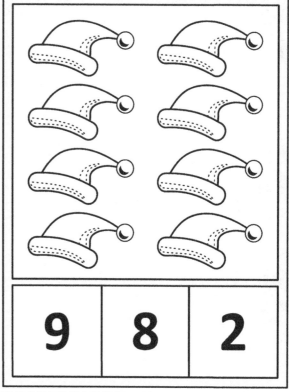

| 9 | 8 | 2 |
|---|---|---|

# COUNT AND COLOR
## (BASED ON THE NUMBER ON THE LEFT)

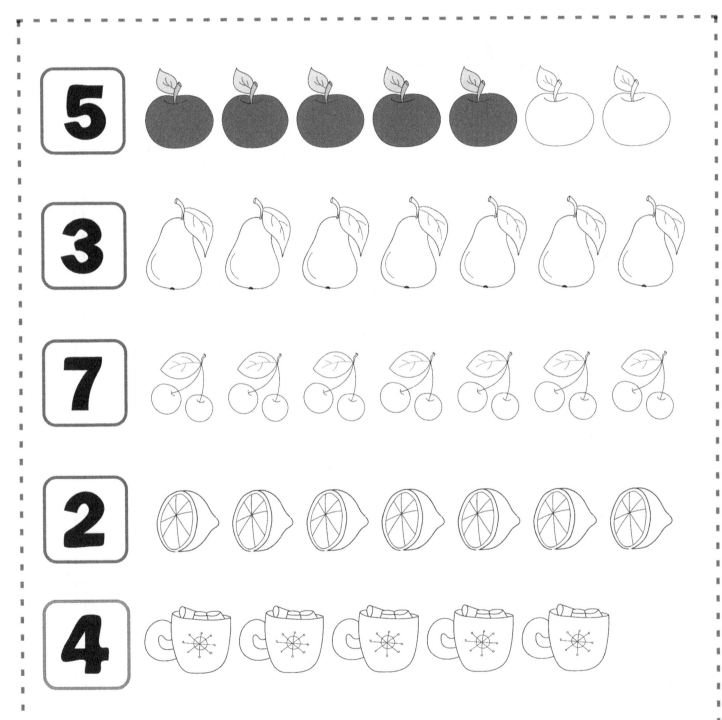

# COUNT AND COLOR
## (BASED ON THE NUMBER ON THE LEFT)

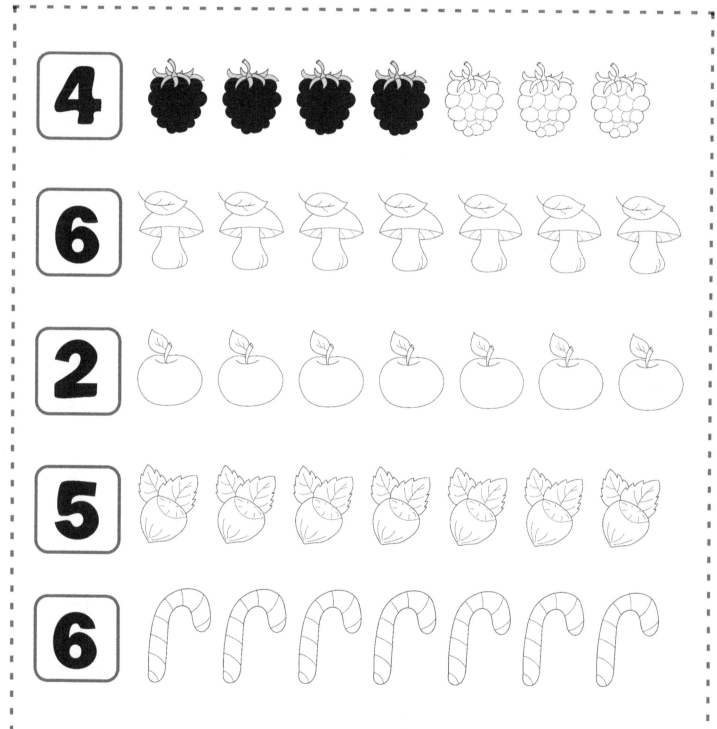

# COUNT AND COLOR
## (BASED ON THE NUMBER ON THE LEFT)

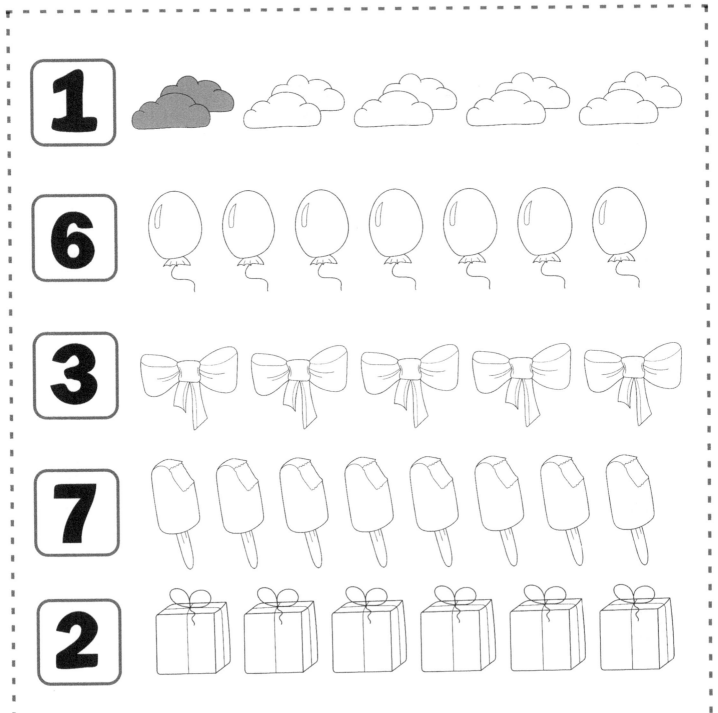

# COUNT AND COLOR
(BASED ON THE NUMBER ON THE LEFT)

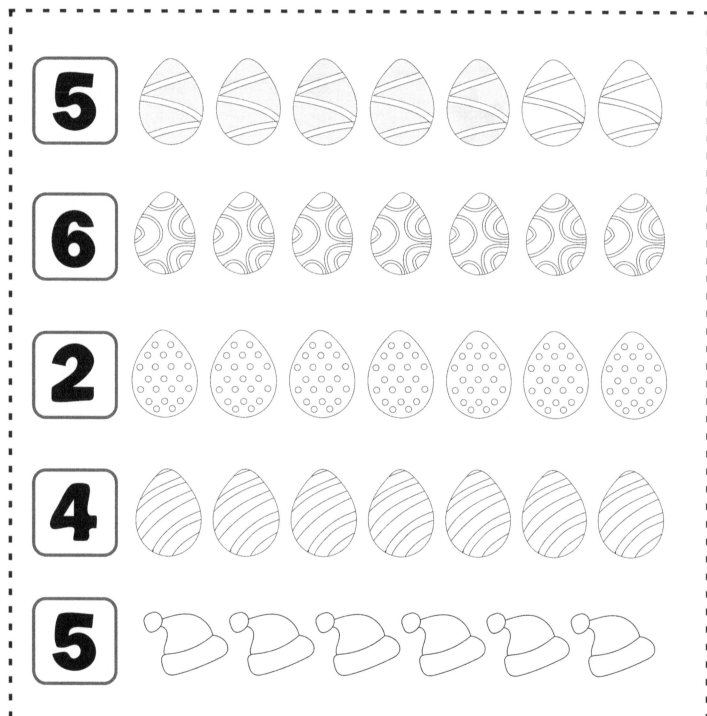

# IT'S TIME FOR COUNTING

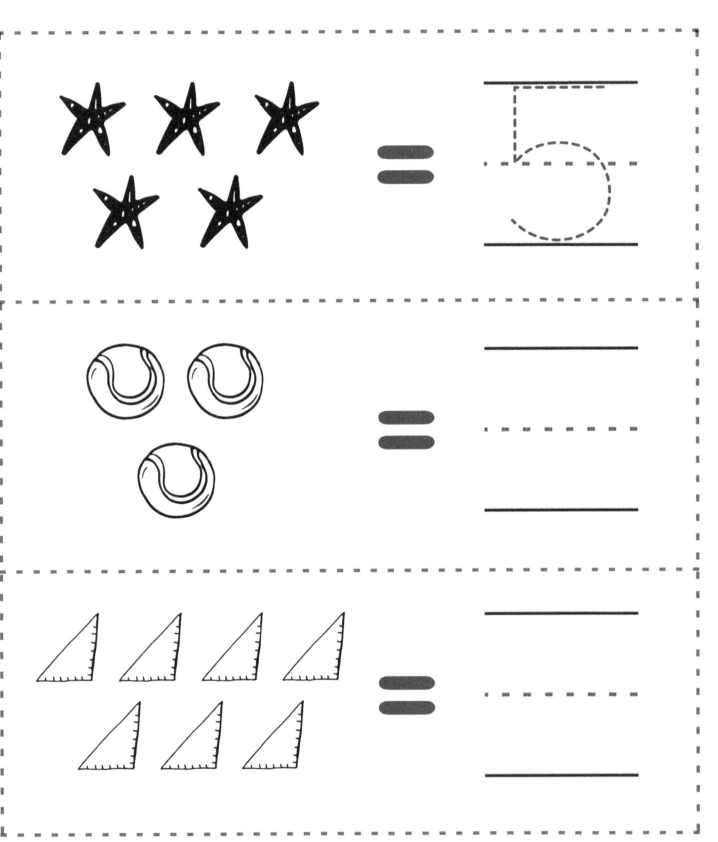

# COUNT HOW MANY ITEMS YOU SEE

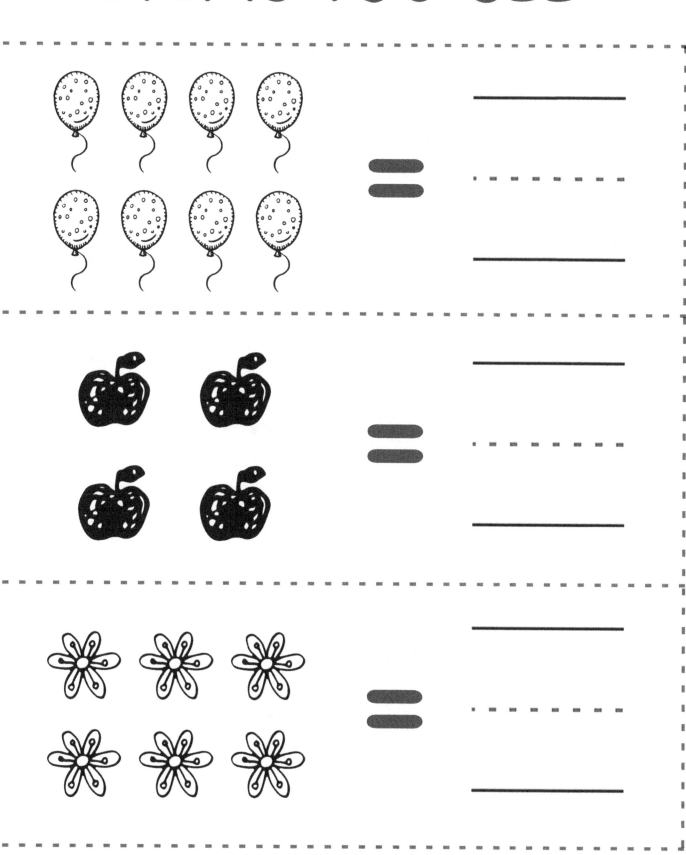

# COUNT HOW MANY ITEMS YOU SEE

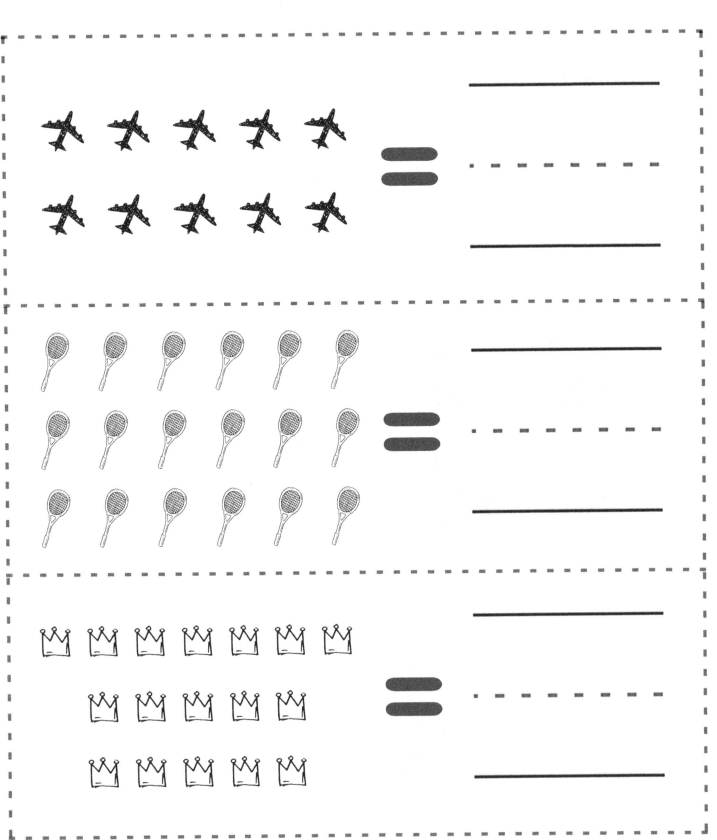

# COUNT HOW MANY ITEMS YOU SEE

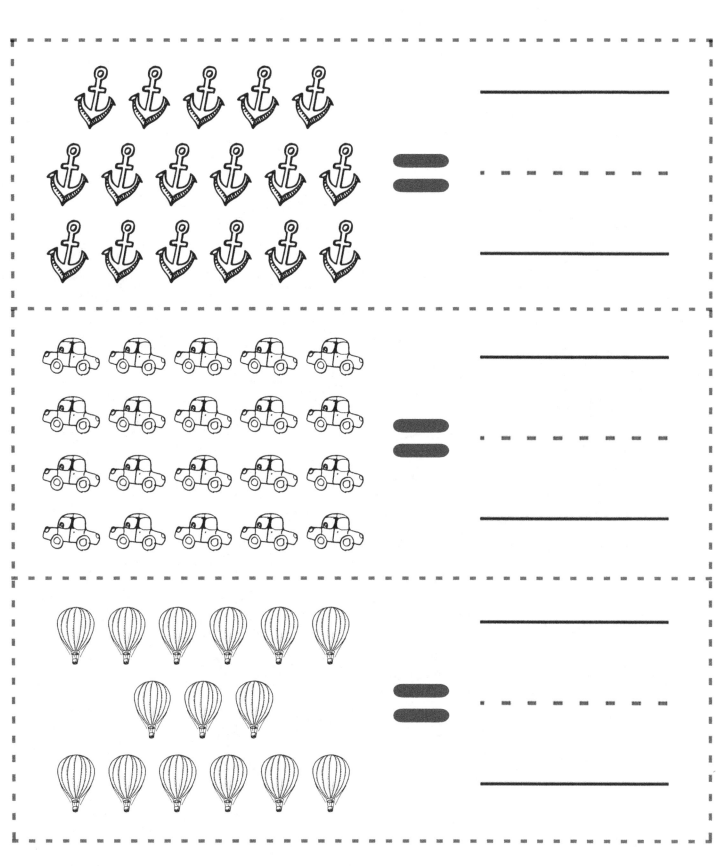

# HOW MANY DINOS DO YOU SEE?

ANSWER HERE

# HOW MANY DONKEYS DO YOU SEE?

# HOW MANY PEOPLE DO YOU SEE?

# HOW MANY HEARTS DO YOU SEE?

# COUNT THE ITEMS
# AND ADD THEM UP

_____

- - - - - - -

_____

_____

- - - - - - -

_____

_____

- - - - - - -

_____

# COUNT THE ITEMS AND ADD THEM UP

| | | | | | |
|---|---|---|---|---|---|
| | + | | = | _____ | |

_____

‑ ‑ ‑ ‑ ‑ ‑

_____

+ =

_____

‑ ‑ ‑ ‑ ‑ ‑

_____

+ =

_____

‑ ‑ ‑ ‑ ‑ ‑

_____

# COUNT THE ITEMS AND ADD THEM UP

_____
- - - - -
_____

_____
- - - - -
_____

_____
- - - - -
_____

# COUNT THE ITEMS AND ADD THEM UP

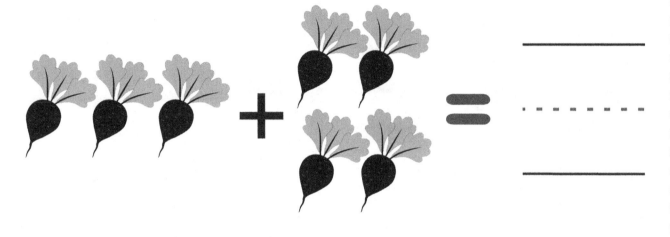

_____

- - - - - - - -

_____

_____

- - - - - - - -

_____

_____

- - - - - - - -

_____

# COUNT THE DOTS AND ADD THEM UP

2 + 2 = 4

3 + 4 = 7

6 + 2 = 8

# COUNT THE DOTS AND ADD THEM UP

1 + 2 = ____

2 + 3 = ____

5 + 1 = ____

# COUNT THE DOTS AND ADD THEM UP

$1 + 1 = $ _____

$4 + 5 = $ _____

$3 + 7 = $ _____

# COUNT THE DOTS AND ADD THEM UP

1 + 8 = _____

3 + 5 = _____

4 + 7 = _____

# SIMPLE ADDITION

(YOU CAN ADD YOUR OWN DOTS BELOW
THE NUMBERS TO MAKE IT EASIER)

$1 + 4 = $ _____

$7 + 1 = $ _____

$6 + 3 = $ _____

# SIMPLE ADDITION

(YOU CAN ADD YOUR OWN DOTS BELOW)
THE NUMBERS TO MAKE IT EASIER

$2 + 7 =$ _____

$5 + 6 =$ _____

$2 + 5 =$ _____

# SIMPLE ADDITION

( YOU CAN ADD YOUR OWN DOTS BELOW
THE NUMBERS TO MAKE IT EASIER )

2 + 4 = _____

8 + 2 = _____

4 + 6 = _____

# SIMPLE ADDITION

(YOU CAN ADD YOUR OWN DOTS BELOW)
THE NUMBERS TO MAKE IT EASIER

1+11 = _____

14+3 = _____

17+2 = _____

# SIMPLE ADDITION

(YOU CAN ADD YOUR OWN DOTS BELOW) THE NUMBERS TO MAKE IT EASIER

5+13 = _____

12+6 = _____

15+4 = _____

# SIMPLE ADDITION

## (YOU CAN ADD YOUR OWN DOTS BELOW
## THE NUMBERS TO MAKE IT EASIER )

2+16 = _____

1+19 = _____

10+4 = _____

# COUNT THE ITEMS AND SUBTRACT THEM

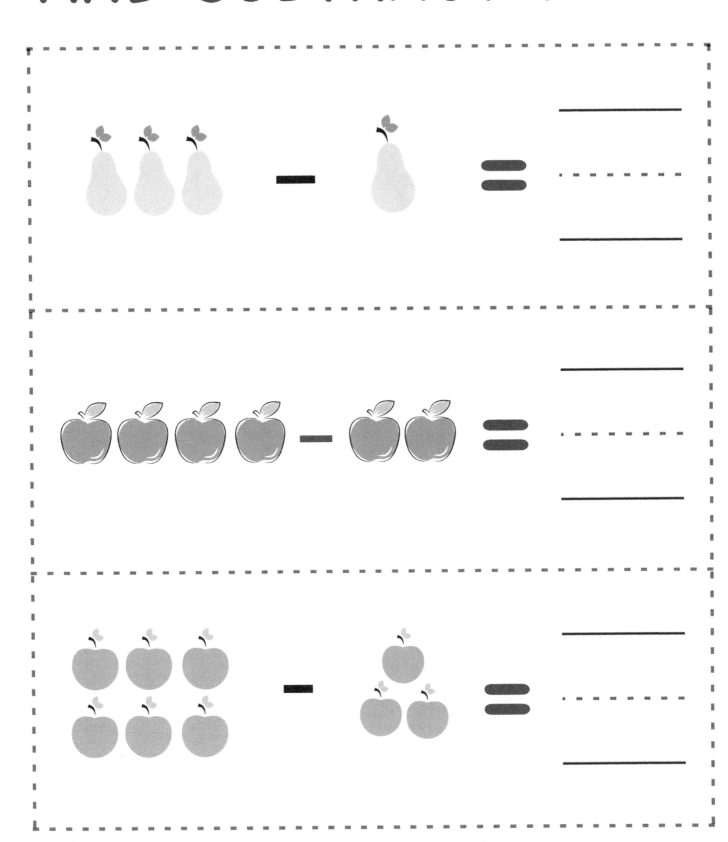

# COUNT THE ITEMS
# AND SUBTRACT THEM

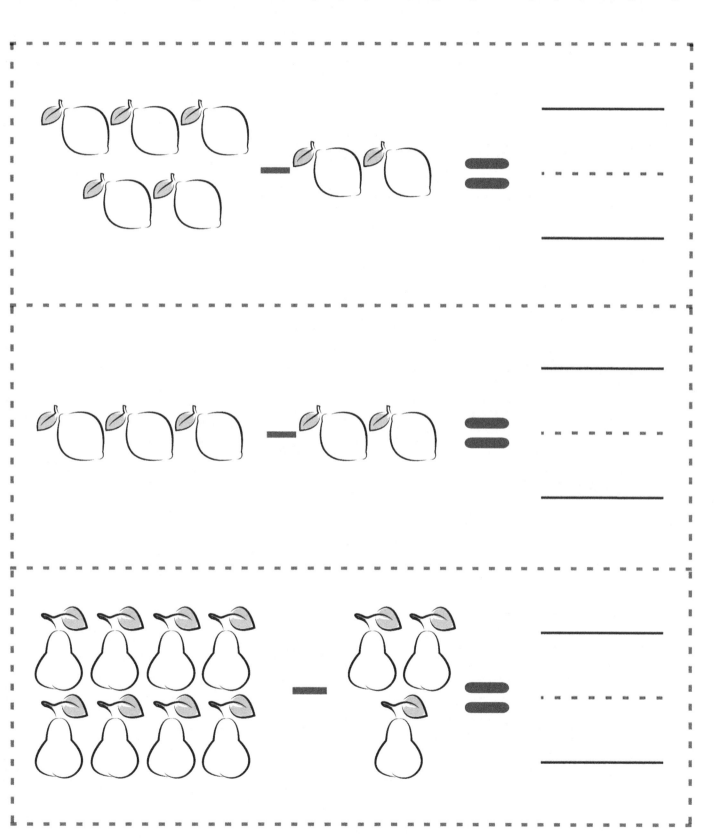

# COUNT THE ITEMS
# AND SUBTRACT THEM

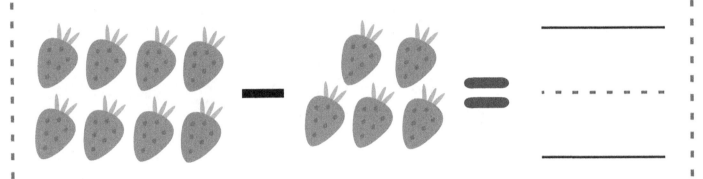

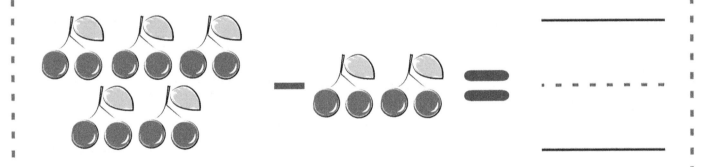

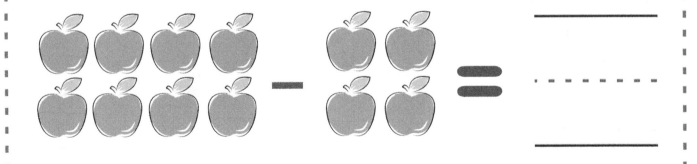

# COUNT THE ITEMS
# AND SUBTRACT THEM

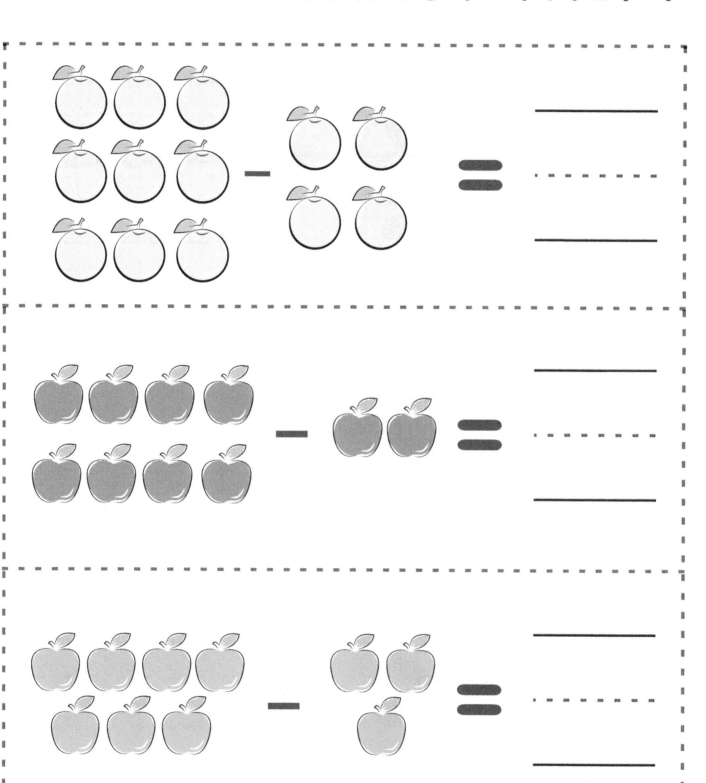

# COUNT THE DOTS AND SUBTRACT THEM

2 - 2 = 0

4 - 3 = 1

6 - 2 = 4

# COUNT THE DOTS AND SUBTRACT THEM

$4 - 2 =$ _____

$7 - 2 =$ _____

$5 - 2 =$ _____

# COUNT THE DOTS AND SUBTRACT THEM

8 - 1 = _____

7 - 1 = _____

7 - 3 = _____

# COUNT THE DOTS AND SUBTRACT THEM

9 - 4 = ____

8 - 7 = ____

5 - 5 = ____

# SIMPLE SUBTRACTION
(YOU CAN ADD YOUR OWN DOTS BELOW)
THE NUMBERS TO MAKE IT EASIER

4 - 1 = _____

5 - 4 = _____

6 - 4 = _____

# SIMPLE SUBTRACTION

(YOU CAN ADD YOUR OWN DOTS BELOW)
THE NUMBERS TO MAKE IT EASIER

7 - 5 = _____

10 - 1 = _____

9 - 3 = _____

# SIMPLE SUBTRACTION
(YOU CAN ADD YOUR OWN DOTS BELOW)
THE NUMBERS TO MAKE IT EASIER

11 - 3 = _____

8 - 4 = _____

7 - 6 = _____

# SIMPLE SUBTRACTION

(YOU CAN ADD YOUR OWN DOTS BELOW)
THE NUMBERS TO MAKE IT EASIER

$14-4 =$ _____

$16-12 =$ _____

$20-9 =$ _____

# SIMPLE SUBTRACTION
( YOU CAN ADD YOUR OWN DOTS BELOW )
THE NUMBERS TO MAKE IT EASIER

13-5 = _____

12-6 = _____

15-6 = _____

# SIMPLE SUBTRACTION
## ( YOU CAN ADD YOUR OWN DOTS BELOW )
## THE NUMBERS TO MAKE IT EASIER

16-2 = _____

19-1 = _____

18-4 = _____

# GET OUT OF THE MAZE GOING 1-10

| 1 | 2 | 3 | 4 |
|---|---|---|---|
| 2 | 5 | 4 | 5 |
| 3 | 6 | 9 | 10 |
| 4 | 7 | 8 | 7 |

# GET OUT OF THE MAZE GOING 1-10

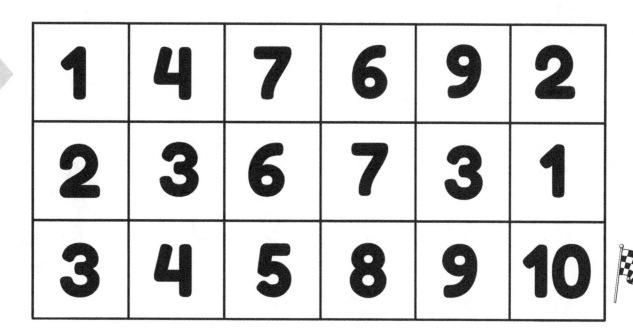

# GET OUT OF THE MAZE GOING 1-15

| | 1 | 2 | 3 | 28 | 80 | 48 | 98 |
|---|---|---|---|---|---|---|---|
| | 79 | 57 | 4 | 5 | 6 | 58 | 90 |
| | 1 | 14 | 3 | 27 | 7 | 8 | 30 |
| 31 | 32 | 33 | 34 | 35 | 36 | 37 | 8 | 9 | 10 |
| 41 | 42 | 43 | 44 | 45 | 46 | 47 | 9 | 49 | 11 |
| 88 | 26 | 53 | 14 | 13 | 12 | 26 | 14 | 13 | 12 |
| 61 | 62 | 63 | 15 | 65 | 66 | 67 | 15 | 69 | 70 |
| 74 | 72 | 73 | 16 | 17 | 18 | 77 | | | |
| 81 | 82 | 83 | 84 | 85 | 19 | 20 | | | |
| 91 | 64 | 93 | 94 | 95 | 96 | 97 | | | |

# GET OUT OF THE MAZE GOING 1-22

| | | 38 | 24 | 78 | 28 | 80 | 48 | 98 |
|---|---|---|---|---|---|---|---|---|
| | | 79 | 57 | 8 | 9 | 10 | 58 | 90 |
| | | 1 | 2 | 7 | 27 | 11 | 12 | 30 |
| 31 | 32 | 1 | 34 | 5 | 6 | 37 | 8 | 13 | 40 |
| 41 | 42 | 2 | 3 | 4 | 46 | 47 | 15 | 14 | 50 |
| 88 | 26 | 53 | 14 | 13 | 12 | 17 | 16 | 59 | 60 |
| 61 | 62 | 63 | 15 | 65 | 19 | 18 | 68 | 69 | 70 |
| 74 | 72 | 73 | 16 | 17 | 20 | 77 | | | |
| 81 | 82 | 83 | 84 | 85 | 21 | 22 | | | |
| 91 | 64 | 93 | 94 | 95 | 96 | 97 | | | |

# GET OUT OF THE MAZE BY DRAWING A LINE THROUGH THE BOXES THAT HAVE SUM OF 50

(NOTE: THIS IS A VERY HARD TASK, SO ONLY TRY IT WHEN YOUR KID IS VERY COMFORTABLE WITH THE REST OF THIS WORKBOOK)

| 15 +29 | 15 +17 | 73 +12 | 22 +55 | 43 + 3 | 11 +44 | 11 +39 | |
| 16 +61 | 16 +34 | 12 +55 | 44 + 6 | 23 + 8 | 4 +46 | 12 +38 | 78 +11 |
| 26 +24 | 26 +24 | 1 +49 = 50 | | | 54 +13 | 10 +40 | 28 +22 |
| 15 +35 | 16 +43 | 18 +15 | | | 2 +88 | 17 +28 | 17 +33 |
| 23 +27 | 42 + 8 | 38 +20 | 3 +54 | 19 + 8 | 25 +40 | 6 +44 | 16 +34 |
| 53 +15 | 20 +30 | 31 +19 | 36 +19 | 4 +46 | 24 +26 | 43 + 7 | 57 +16 |
| 19 +35 | 21 +13 | 5 +45 | 36 +14 | 4 +46 | 24 +21 | 57 +16 | 33 +23 |

# GET OUT OF THE MAZE BY DRAWING A LINE THROUGH THE BOXES THAT HAVE SUM OF 100

(NOTE: THIS IS A VERY HARD TASK, SO ONLY TRY IT WHEN YOUR KID IS VERY COMFORTABLE WITH THE REST OF THIS WORKBOOK)

| 32 + 68 | 15 + 85 | 73 + 27 | 22 + 34 | 43 + 57 | 35 + 40 | 11 + 89 | → |
|---------|---------|---------|---------|---------|---------|---------|---|
| 16 + 84 | 16 + 62 | 42 + 58 | 38 + 61 | 3 + 97 | 19 + 58 | 25 + 75 | 6 + 33 |
| 26 + 74 | 13 + 82 | 25 + 75 = 100 | ← | | 36 + 31 | 4 + 96 | 24 + 17 |
| 15 + 85 | 16 + 43 | 18 + 57 | | | 2 + 73 | 17 + 83 | 17 + 83 |
| 23 + 77 | 42 + 58 | 38 + 20 | 14 + 43 | 7 + 20 | 25 + 40 | 6 + 42 | 16 + 84 |
| 17 + 58 | 12 + 88 | 31 + 44 | 36 + 64 | 4 + 96 | 24 + 76 | 43 + 22 | 57 + 43 |
| 43 + 45 | 21 + 79 | 5 + 95 | 36 + 64 | 4 + 79 | 24 + 76 | 57 + 43 | 33 + 67 |

Made in the USA
Coppell, TX
28 March 2020